EXTREMELY Weird ANIMALS

PROBOSCIS MONKEY

BY LISA OWINGS

BELLWETHER MEDIA • MINNEAPOLIS, MN

Jump into the cockpit and take flight with Pilot books. Your journey will take you on high-energy adventures as you learn about all that is wild, weird, fascinating, and fun!

This edition first published in 2014 by Bellwether Media, Inc.

Library of Congress Cataloging-in-Publication Data

Owings, Lisa.
  Proboscis Monkey / by Lisa Owings.
    pages cm. – (Pilot: Extremely Weird Animals)
  Summary: "Engaging images accompany information about proboscis monkeys. The combination of high-interest subject matter and narrative text is intended for students in grades 3 through 7"– Provided by publisher.
  Audience: Ages 7-12.
  Includes bibliographical references and index.
  ISBN 978-1-62617-077-3 (hardcover : alk. paper)
  1. Proboscis monkey–Juvenile literature. I. Title.
  QL737.P93O95 2014
  599.8'6–dc23
                          2013038528

Printed in the United States of America, North Mankato, MN.

TABLE OF CONTENTS

A CLOSE CALL

The light is fading from the skies over Borneo. A male proboscis monkey leads his group of females toward the river to sleep. They settle in the leafy branches that hang over the water. Holding their young close, the females get comfortable for the night. The male keeps watch over them. He scans the area for signs of danger.

The male is about to fall asleep. Suddenly, he sees movement in the branches nearby. He catches a glimpse of spotted fur. A clouded leopard is racing through the trees toward one of the mothers and her baby. The male calls out in alarm. With each raspy honk, his bulb of a nose swells to help his voice carry. The mother hears him. She sees the threat just in time. With her baby clinging tightly to her chest, she leaps out of the way. The family is safe, at least for tonight.

A PECULIAR PRIMATE

The proboscis monkey is a very strange-looking mammal. The male has a large, bulb-shaped nose that dangles over his mouth. The female also has a large nose. Hers is shorter and sticks straight out. All proboscis monkeys have big, round bellies. The male is about twice as large as the female. He can weigh up to 50 pounds (23 kilograms). Minus his tail, the male can reach nearly 30 inches (76 centimeters) in length.

The adult proboscis monkey has a pink face. Its fur deepens from pale orange around the neck and chest to reddish brown on the head and back. The fur around its long arms and legs is gray. The proboscis monkey's white tail is about as long as its body. This long tail helps it keep its balance in trees.

human

proboscis
monkey

Baby Blues

Baby proboscis monkeys have blue faces and upturned noses.

Like all other monkeys, the proboscis monkey is a primate. It is part of the family Cercopithecidae, which is made up of Old World monkeys. These monkeys have nostrils that point downward. They also have tails that are unable to grip branches. Old World monkeys are divided into two groups. Proboscis monkeys belong to the leaf-eating group, called Colobinae. They are the only members of the genus *Nasalis*.

Proboscis monkeys are found only on the island of Borneo in Southeast Asia. The countries of Indonesia, Malaysia, and Brunei share this large island in the Pacific Ocean. The weather on Borneo is hot and damp. Proboscis monkeys live in forests along the coast or near rivers and swamps. They rarely stray far from the water.

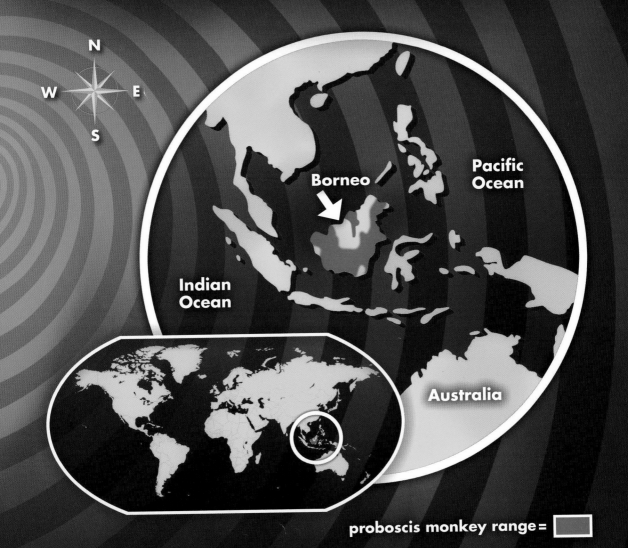

Pacific Ocean

Borneo

Indian Ocean

Australia

proboscis monkey range =

In the mornings and evenings, they climb through the treetops in search of leaves and fruits. Sometimes they eat flowers or seeds. They hardly ever come down from the trees.

Proboscis monkeys travel in groups called harems. Most harems include one adult male, several females, and their young. The male watches over the group. Males that are not old enough to breed travel in all-male groups. Multiple groups sometimes join together to form troops. They do this most often at night.

Several predators attack proboscis monkeys. Crocodiles and false gavials lurk in the rivers, waiting to snap at slow-moving monkeys. Clouded leopards are rare but deadly. These large cats move almost as easily through the trees as monkeys do. They usually prey on young proboscis monkeys. However, they sometimes attack adults. Humans also kill proboscis monkeys for food or to keep them from eating their crops.

Medicine or Madness?

People also hunt proboscis monkeys for stone-like objects called bezoars. These are sometimes found in the monkeys' intestines. Some believe bezoars have healing powers.

BIG NOSES AND BELLY FLOPS

Proboscis monkeys have longer noses than any other primate. The male's nose can grow up to 7 inches (17.5 centimeters) long. Adult males have to push their noses out of the way when they eat. Their noses also flop around as they move.

Scientists believe these odd noses help proboscis monkeys attract and defend mates. The male's large nose makes his call sound louder. Female monkeys seem to prefer larger noses and louder calls. That means the larger a male's nose is, the better chance he has to start his own harem. Once he has one, he can use his giant nose and noisy honking to scare off other males. The male's loud call also makes it easy for him to warn his mates of nearby threats.

Red Alert
It is easy to tell when a male proboscis monkey is angry or excited. His nose turns red and gets even larger.

The proboscis monkey's nose is not the only oversized part of its body. Its round belly sticks out as if there were a basketball inside. This belly has an important purpose. Proboscis monkeys need big stomachs to help them digest leaves.

The proboscis monkey's stomach has four parts. The first two parts are filled with special bacteria that break down leaves. The other two parts help the proboscis monkey absorb the nutrients from its food. Proboscis monkeys sometimes regurgitate their food and chew it again. This may speed up their digestion and allow them to eat more. Cows and camels also eat like this.

Sour Fruit

Proboscis monkeys eat only unripe fruits. The sugars in ripe fruits cause gas to build up in their stomachs. This problem, called bloat, can be deadly.

Proboscis monkeys often cross rivers in search of food. They have to be quick or a crocodile might eat them. If the river is narrow enough, they take a flying leap over it. They use trees to help launch themselves across. First, they use their body weight to get a tree or branch swaying. Then they take a big leap as the tree swings them toward the other side.

The monkeys stretch their arms in front of them as they fly through the air. They try to catch hold of a branch on the other side of the river. Sometimes they do not make it all the way. Instead, they land in the river with a huge belly flop! They quickly climb out of the water and back into the trees.

Hold On Tight
Mother proboscis monkeys often leap across rivers with their babies holding on for dear life!

Proboscis monkeys are great swimmers when they have to be. To cross wide rivers, they must slide quietly through the water because splashing can attract crocodiles. The monkeys gently lower themselves into the water. Then they dog-paddle to the other side. Their hands and feet are partly webbed. This makes it easy for them to swim quickly. It also helps keep them from sinking in the mud. Groups of proboscis monkeys often swim across rivers in single file.

The monkeys use water to escape from leopards and other land predators. As soon as they see a threat, they dive from the trees. Proboscis monkeys can stay hidden underwater for a long time. They can swim for more than 65 feet (20 meters) without coming up for air.

Walking Like We Do

In shallow water, proboscis monkeys often wade on two feet. They keep their hands and arms above the water. Sometimes they even walk this way on land.

IN NEED OF PROTECTION

Proboscis monkeys are in danger. People are cutting down the trees proboscis monkeys live in for homes and farmland. The monkeys are still hunted for meat or bezoars, too. Forest fires and pollution harm the monkeys and their habitat. In recent years, more than half of Borneo's proboscis monkeys have died out. They are now an endangered species.

Bornean countries have passed laws to protect proboscis monkeys. Groups of monkeys can be found in at least 16 wildlife reserves and national parks across the island. People must work together to protect their wild habitat and save these strange and wonderful animals.

EXTINCT

EXTINCT IN THE WILD

CRITICALLY ENDANGERED

ENDANGERED

VULNERABLE

NEAR THREATENED

LEAST CONCERN

Proboscis Monkey
Fact File

Common Name:	proboscis monkey
Scientific Name:	*Nasalis larvatus*
Nickname:	long-nosed monkey
Famous Features:	large nose, big stomach
Distribution:	Borneo
Habitats:	forests near rivers, coastlines, and swamps
Diet:	leaves, fruits, seeds, flowers, insects
Life Span:	13 years in the wild
Current Status:	endangered

GLOSSARY

absorb—to soak up or take in

bacteria—very tiny, single-celled organisms that can either be useful or cause disease

breed—to mate to produce young

digest—to break down food so that it can be used by the body

endangered—at risk of becoming extinct

genus—a group of similar species

harems—small family groups of proboscis monkeys

mammal—an animal that has a backbone, hair, and feeds its young milk

nutrients—parts of food that provide energy

Old World—referring to Europe, Asia, and Africa

pollution—harmful substances that affect an environment

primate—a member of a group of mammals that can use their hands to grasp food and other objects; lemurs, monkeys, apes, and humans are examples of primates.

proboscis—a big, long nose

regurgitate—to bring food that has been eaten from the stomach up into the mouth

threat—possible danger

troops—groups of proboscis monkey harems that live together

webbed—having thin skin connecting fingers and toes

wildlife reserves—areas where animals are protected and cannot be hunted

TO LEARN MORE

AT THE LIBRARY

Aloian, Molly, and Bobbie Kalman. *Endangered Monkeys*.
New York, N.Y.: Crabtree Pub. Co., 2007.

Stefoff, Rebecca. *The Primate Order*. New York, N.Y.: Marshall
Cavendish Benchmark, 2006.

Wojahn, Rebecca Hogue. *A Mangrove Forest Food Chain:
A Who-Eats-What Adventure in Asia*. Minneapolis, Minn.:
Lerner Publications, 2010.

ON THE WEB

Learning more about proboscis monkeys
is as easy as 1, 2, 3.

1. Go to www.factsurfer.com.

2. Enter "proboscis monkeys" into
   the search box.

3. Click the "Surf" button and you
   will see a list of related Web sites.

With factsurfer.com, finding more information
is just a click away.

INDEX

The images in this book are reproduced through the courtesy of: Ronald van der Beek, front cover; Berendje Photography, p. 5; J & C Sohns/ Tier und Naturfotografie/ SuperStock, p. 7; Mejini Neskah, p. 8; Peter Lilja/ agefotostock, pp. 10-11; Cuson, p. 13; Minden Pictures/ SuperStock, p. 14; McPhoto/ agefotostock, p. 15; Anup Shah/ Nature Picture Library, pp. 16-17; Fiona Rogers/ Corbis, p. 18; LightRocket/ Getty Images, p. 19; BlueOrange Studio, p. 21.